IMAGES
of America

TIVERTON AND
LITTLE COMPTON

RHODE ISLAND

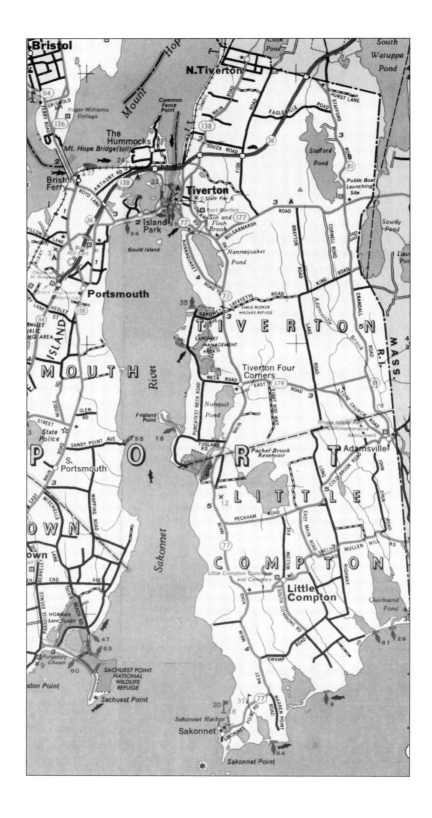

IMAGES
of America

TIVERTON AND LITTLE COMPTON

RHODE ISLAND

POCASSET AND SAKONNET, WAMPANOAG COUNTRY

Nancy Jensen Devin and Richard V. Simpson

ARCADIA

First published 1997
Copyright © Nancy Jensen Devin and Richard V. Simpson, 1997

ISBN 0-7524-0577-2

Published by Arcadia Publishing,
an imprint of the Chalford Publishing Corporation,
One Washington Center, Dover, New Hampshire 03820.
Printed in Great Britain

Library of Congress Cataloging-in-Publication Data applied for

Other Publications by R.V. Simpson:

*Crown of Gold: A History of the Italian-Roman Catholic
Church in Bristol, RI* (1967)

Independence Day: How the Day is Celebrated in Bristol, RI (1989)
Old St. Mary's: Mother Church in Bristol, RI (1994)

Bristol, Rhode Island: In the Mount Hope Lands of King Philip (1996)

A Book by N.J. Devin and R.V. Simpson:

Portsmouth, Rhode Island: Pocasset: Ancestral Lands of the Narragansett (1997)

Dedicated to the Squaw Sachems Weetamoe and Awashonks.

Contents

Pocasset Purchase. Judging by the prospect of Mount Hope Bay, this view encompasses the portion of North Tiverton set off to Fall River in 1862. This image is a *c.* 1880 chromolithograph titled *View of Mount Hope Bay, Rhode Island* after G. Dubois; published by H.W. Dubois & Co., Fall River, Massachusetts.

Introduction

When colonists arrived at Plymouth in 1620, the Wampanoag country extended from Narragansett Bay to Cape Cod. At the death of Massasoit in 1661, the Indian lands were reduced to Montaup (Mount Hope Neck), Pocasset (Tiverton), and Sakonnet* (Little Compton).

The easternmost part of Rhode Island consists of a narrow strip of land contained between the Massachusetts line on the east and the Sakonnet River and Mount Hope Bay on the west. In area it is about 10 miles long from north to south, and only about 3.5 miles wide. A portion of Tiverton was given over to Fall River in 1862 in the settlement of a boundary dispute between Massachusetts and Rhode Island.

Tiverton

Like its neighboring town, Little Compton, Tiverton was governed by a Wampanoag squaw sachem. Weetamoe ruled as queen of the Pocasset tribe; she joined with the Great Sachem Metacom (King Philip) in his struggle against the colonists. However, the squaw sachem of the Soughkonnets, Awashonks, remained neutral during the "war."

In 1629, Plymouth Colony's Governor Bradford purchased Pocasset from its original inhabitants. Shortly after King Philip's War, in 1680, Plymouth Governor Winslow then sold the lands to Edward Gray and seven other Englishmen for the sum of £1,200. A portion of the first Tiverton settlement was known as "Pocasset Purchase." The southern portion of the town was sometimes known by its native name, Punkatust. Eventually, the principal settlements became known as North Tiverton, Tiverton, and Tiverton Four Corners.

6

Tiverton was incorporated as a township in 1694. By royal decree in 1746, Tiverton, along with Little Compton, Bristol, Warren, and Cumberland, was brought within the jurisdiction of Rhode Island. For approximately three years during the Revolution when the British held Aquidneck Island, Tiverton was an asylum for Americans fleeing from British oppression.

At Tiverton Heights, above the old Stone Bridge, are the remains of Fort Barton. There a force of 10,000 armed Americans garrisoned during the British occupancy of Newport. From this point the Americans under General Sullivan crossed over to Portsmouth in movements that led to the Battle of Rhode Island on August 29, 1778. Because Sullivan's assault on Portsmouth was launched from Tiverton, the ensuing encounter with the British is locally referred to as the Battle of Tiverton Heights. Remnants of the old Stone Bridge connection to Aquidneck Island remain near the middle of the Pocasset lands, at Tiverton; just south of this center is an almost landlocked inlet named Nanaquaket Pond. Most of the oldest houses of the settlement are found along this waterfront road.

Of the notable men whose names are associated with Tiverton's history, perhaps the most prominent is Joseph Wanton. Wanton was one of the most successful shipbuilders in the colony, and many of the famous merchantmen and privateers of the time were launched from his yard.

Cotton and woolen mills were established as early as 1827. Until 1900, Tiverton's chief industries involved boat construction, agriculture, and fishing interests. The bountiful Narragansett Bay was responsible for a prosperous fishing industry. The water's yield of an abundance of menhaden fish resulted in the establishment of processing factories for the production of industrial oil and fertilizer. Today, fewer than 1,500 of Tiverton's 14,400 residents work at local trade establishments, the town's major employers.

Since the last quarter of the 1800s, the town's Sakonnet River shore has become a favorite summer resort. Recent residential development is concentrated in the North Tiverton area. The picturesque village of Tiverton Four Corners clusters around the junction of West Main Road and East Road. Here, the industrial and urban sprawl to the north are forgotten. Green fields stretch down to the shore of the bay; it is surely one of the most picturesque corners of Newport County.

Little Compton

From its earliest history, the territory covered by this town was inhabited by the Soughkonnets. As a sub-tribe of the Wampanoags, at the time of the area's settlement by the whites they were under the dominion of Queen Awashonks, widely known as the "Squaw Sachem." It was from Awashonks that Constant Southworth and others received the deed to a large tract of land in the westerly part of the town on July 30, 1673. Thus, the first settlement in the area was led in 1674 by (Captain) Benjamin Church of Duxbury, a carpenter who is known as the vanquisher of King Philip. Sometime after 1680, Church settled in Bristol and died there in 1718.

Shortly after the establishment of this settlement, King Philip of Pokanoket began trying to unite all the Native Americans in the New England area in an effort to drive the whites from their territory. Captain Church, a ruthless fighter and a wily diplomat, hearing of this threat, boldly visited Awashonks at her camp; there he met the emissaries of King Philip. In the presence of Philip's men, Church convinced Awashonks to remain neutral in the events to follow.

In the period following King Philip's War the town became more fully settled, although it remained a quiet, rural community composed primarily of agricultural and fishing interests. The settlers from Plymouth were mainly Congregationalists. The town meetinghouse they built on the Commons in 1693 was both a Congregational meetinghouse and a town hall. A small group of Quakers from Aquidneck Island were the second group of settlers here. Their meetinghouse, erected c. 1700, was the first building used solely for religious purposes.

Looming over Little Compton Commons on Meeting House Lane stands the United

Congregational Church. The burial ground, laid out in 1675–77, contains several monuments of interest. Among them is one to Elizabeth Pabodie, the first white woman born in the colonies (daughter of John and Priscilla Mullins Alden); another is at the grave of Benjamin Church.

During the British occupation of Aquidneck Island, an outpost of the patriot army was stationed in this town. Foraging parties from the British garrison invaded Little Compton several times. The British raiders met with stiff resistance from the settlers, and were "bushwhacked" several times as in the locally celebrated skirmish at the Taggart House.

Whenever word of proposed British troop movement came to Isaac Barker of Middletown, he placed a message describing the movement under a certain rock on the shore, and then set a signal on high land. The patriots at Little Compton, seeing the signal, would cross the Sakonnet River in the night, take the concealed message, and transmit its contents to the commander of the American forces.

Adamsville, named after John Adams, is distinctly different in character from the rest of Little Compton. The village nestles in a deep valley between wooded ridges sloping southward to the head of the Acoaxet River. Because of the difficulty in plowing stony fields, the community turned its back on farming and joined its neighbor Westport, Massachusetts, to form a social and economic unit. Whaling and trading vessels sailed up the Acoaxet; during Prohibition the hidden channels of the river and the high overviews of rolling landscape provided an advantage to rumrunners, thus earning the area the name "Valley of Sin."

Today, Little Compton is a rural farming community of about 3,500 full-time residents. Fishing is still a major industry in the town, as one can observe by the daily comings and goings of the fishing fleet from the Sakonnet Point wharf.

Summary

No manufacturing or large commercial interests have settled the Pocasset and Sakonnet lands. Since about 1880, the towns' agricultural communities and fishing ports have become popular locations of resort areas and summer homes. Verdant pastures rolling to the shore and the cries of sea birds mingling with the roar of the breakers on the rock-bound coast are the sights and sounds familiar to the local residents. This narrow strip on Rhode Island's eastern flank forms one of the most peaceful, beautiful, and remote corners of the state; it retains the traditional atmosphere of Colonial New England.

For an in-depth perspective on the development of Rhode Island's East Bay, the reader is directed to these books in Arcadia's Images of America series: *Bristol, Rhode Island: In the Mount Hope Lands of King Philip* (1996), and *Portsmouth, Rhode Island: Pocasset: Ancestral Lands of the Narragansett* (1997).

*Authors' Note: During research for this book, we found several spellings of both Nanaquaket and Sakonnet, including Nannaquacket, Nanaquackett, Seakonnet, and Soughkonnet. In this history, we have generally used the most common spellings.

One
Between the Bridges:
Stone Bridge Village

The Stone Bridge Historic District. This district is a loosely defined settlement in the relatively narrow area between the railroad bridge in North Tiverton and a rugged upland section to the east. Main Road forms the "spine" of the village, extending from approximately Route 24 in the north to the Quaket River near the Bridgeport Historic District in the south. This c. 1906 photograph and the five following photographs, from the vantage point of the Portsmouth Hummock, form a panoramic view of the village (north to south) between the bridges.

Immediately south of the railroad bridge. The first activity in Tiverton's Stone Bridge area related to the settlement of Portsmouth, when in 1640 a ferry service was established. Soon, Main Road became the most important artery in this settlement; a mixture of dwellings and public facilities, including a marina, the Stone Bridge Cottages, and two churches, sprang up near the Tiverton approach to Stone Bridge.

The Howland Ferry. In 1674, John Simmons built a house and was licensed to keep a public tavern or eating house; he also ran the ferry. The Howland family ran the ferry c. 1700–1776, and thus the settlement on the Tiverton side of the Sakonnet assumed the name Howland's Ferry. The Howland name continued in use well into the nineteenth century.

During the Revolutionary War. The area of Howland's Ferry was an important staging area for several proposed invasions of British-occupied Aquidneck Island. Both Fort Barton and Fort Durfee, constructed by the American Army on the heights overlooking the Sakonnet River and Mount Hope Bay, command an excellent view of the island.

The first Stone Bridge. Originally built in 1794, the bridge was damaged, repaired, destroyed, and rebuilt several times during the following 150 years. Easier communication between Aquidneck and Tiverton encouraged the village's slow but steady growth. Eventually, the cluster of buildings around the bridge became known as Stone Bridge. The Fall River Yacht Club building is in the center behind the pogy boat's smokestack.

Stone Bridge, *c.* 1906. By 1864, the nucleus of about twelve buildings at Stone Bridge Village included a blacksmith, a boot shop, a general store and post office, and a hotel. In 1871, seven cottages occupied the heights; a restaurant and shore dining hall was built near the depot. After fire destroyed Lawton House in 1884, it was rebuilt as the Stone Bridge Cottage (see top left). This resort survived into the third quarter of the 1900s as the Stone Bridge Inn.

A contemporary (November 11, 1996) view of the old Stone Bridge and Stone Bridge Inn from O'Neil's Point. In 1957, after more than a century and a half of service, the Stone Bridge was closed, and soon after, the center portion removed. Its stone abutments are now popular with fishermen. Many of the sites and structures in Tiverton's Stone Bridge area are historically and architecturally important.

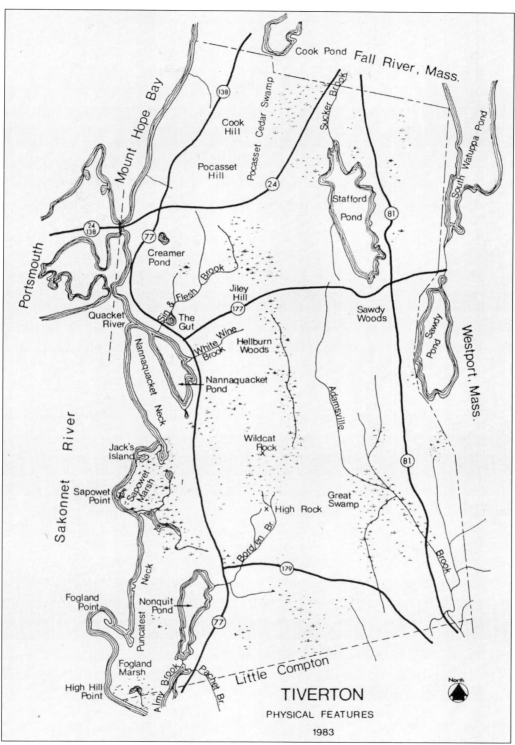

A detail map of Tiverton, Rhode Island.

13

The old Stone Bridge with wooden draw raised, c. 1904. Before the first bridge was built between Tiverton and Portsmouth, a ferry navigated the narrow breadth of the Sakonnet between the two settlements called Pocasset. Besides Howland's Ferry, in 1738 a ferry ran from Fogland Point to Glen Road in Portsmouth.

A bird's-eye view of Stone Bridge Village from the Nanaquaket water tower, c. 1909. In the left background is Hummock Point, Portsmouth; the large outcrop of rock is The Hummock. In the left middle-ground is the approach to the Stone Bridge and in the center is the Stone Bridge Cottage.

The Tiverton approach to the old Stone Bridge, *c.* 1906. Howland's Ferry operated here until about 1794. In 1795 a toll bridge was built and operated by the Rhode Island Bridge Company; it was operated sporadically thereafter. The river's strong current and several severe storms destroyed the bridge a number of times, but it was always rebuilt with improved technology.

A *c.* 1906 view south to Nanaquaket and the Nathaniel Boomer Church House from the Stone Bridge causeway. Tolls were eliminated in 1871 when the Stone Bridge was purchased by the towns of Tiverton and Portsmouth and then given to the state of Rhode Island.

A view of the "modern" 1907 steel draw. Construction of the proposed Newport and Fall River Street Railway required replacement of the old wooden draw with a more substantial iron and steel structure. The new bridge provided a 20-foot-wide roadway capable of supporting 20 tons. In 1898, the new draw was installed and the first trolley traversed the span on June 18.

The Rhode Island Stone Bridge as it appeared in July 1907. The bridge and its approaches suffered severe damage due to strong tidal flow and violent storms. Between 1904 and 1907, a replacement bridge was built; it was wider and provided greater channel clearance.

No. 1393-B Stone Bridge Ti R.I.

A sweeping view of the state-owned Stone Bridge and its east and west approaches. A new double-roller lift bridge was opened for traffic in 1907. Until then, because of disruptive—albeit temporary—closings of the older bridge, the Rhode Island State Division of Highways provided a free ferry service.

The Portsmouth approach to the Stone Bridge. The bridge survived, with interruptions due to ship collision damage and the hurricanes of 1938 and 1954, until May 6, 1957, when it was officially closed and the central span removed after 163 years of service. Travelers now use the Sakonnet River Bridge a short distance north, near the steel railroad bridge.

The Tiverton approach. This 1906 image and the one opposite (p. 19, top) form a panoramic view of the Tiverton approach to the Sakonnet River Railroad Bridge. The actual railroad depot was farther east (see Images of America: *Portsmouth, Rhode Island*). In the background, on the Portsmouth side, the escarpment called The Hummock can be clearly seen.

A view of the railroad depot (right) from the railroad bridge. The 1898 Sakonnet River Railroad Bridge is a modified Baltimore through-truss span and cantilevered assembly about 200 feet long, and is composed of two identical trusses. The circular track on which the bridge pivots is mounted on a central pier in mid-river.

The Tiverton approach to the railroad bridge. In the background is the Church brothers' Portsmouth fish-processing factory. The first railroad bridge over the Sakonnet River was built in 1864 by the Old Colony and Newport Railroad. It was damaged in 1898 and replaced by the present bridge.

The north end of Stone Bridge Village, c. 1900. Railroad passenger service was provided to Aquidneck Island until 1937. In the twentieth century, the line was owned by the New York, New Haven and Hartford Railroad. Conrail now owns the right-of-way, and except for an occasional freight run, the tracks are seldom used and the central bridge span remains open to river traffic.

The view immediately west of the railroad bridge, c. 1900. The water's edge, lined with fishermen's shanties and fish markets, docks for clam diggers and boats to let, presented a colorful face to vacationers. The busy waterfront between the bridges and beyond attracted summer residents who transformed Tiverton Heights, Nanaquaket, and several other parts of town into fashionable neighborhoods.

Below the railroad bridge, Riverside Drive and Evens Avenue, c. 1900–1910 (see p. 18, top). The two buildings at right still exist. The building at the far right is in an advanced state of neglect. In 1993 the large building in the center housed Riverside Marine. Today it is a bait shop.

Two

On, Above, and Around the Sakonnet River

A panoramic series. This c. 1907 photograph and the following four form a panoramic view of the Sakonnet River, Mount Hope Bay, Portsmouth, and Bristol Ferry from Fort Barton on the heights above the narrow passage. Gould Island, known as Owl's Nest during Colonial times, is marked with an 'X'. Tiverton was an active participant in the Revolutionary War, when the British occupied Aquidneck Island, from 1776 to 1779. Fortifications and a lookout station were located on High Hill.

A view from the Baptist church, *c*. 1906. The finger of land with the dozen or so cottages on it is the resort area known as the Hummocks; to the left, in Portsmouth Cove, are the Spectacle Islands. Tiverton's waters were the scenes of two engagements with the British. Fortifications on Gould Island and at Fort Point below Tiverton Heights helped cover American troops being ferried across the Sakonnet.

A *c*. 1906 view from Fort Barton. The ferry *Islander* heads north passing the Hummocks. Note the ferries at the Portsmouth landing of Howland's Ferry. In the background are the rolling fields that eventually became part of Portsmouth Park; the road known as East Main is lined with a row of trees. The Americans gathered at Tiverton Heights enjoyed the same grand perspective of northeast Aquidneck Island.

A view from Fort Barton, *c.* 1906. Menhaden fishing boats at anchor line the Hummock's shore; the large outcropping of rock (right) is The Hummock. Above the cove and the Portsmouth approach to Bristol Ferry are Narragansett Bay and Prudence Island. In October 1777 Major Silas Talbot, in a small sloop, under the cover of darkness, captured the British galley *Pigot* that had been blockading the Sakonnet.

A *c.* 1906 view from Fort Barton. The railroad bridge is hidden by buildings. In the middle ground are the Portsmouth fish-processing factories. The thin finger of land pointing north is Common Fence Point. The Colonial American Army used this commanding view of Mount Hope Bay and Bristol Ferry to good advantage. Mount Hope is the hill in the center background. A few buildings can be seen on the eastern shore of Mount Hope; these may represent the once-popular Mount Hope Amusement Park.

The Fall River Yacht Club, *c.* 1908. After this building was destroyed by the 1938 hurricane, the Tiverton Yacht Club was housed in the present Standish Boat Yard building.

U.S. Navy Wooden Torpedo Boat No. 1 (the Herreshoff-built *Stiletto*) conducts torpedo launching experiments in the Sakonnet River, *c.* 1898. In May 1893, Lieutenant F.H. Paine, representing the Naval Torpedo Station, Newport, contracted Tiverton men to build and maintain a large raft in the Sakonnet River. The raft, from which torpedo experiments were conducted, was nestled in the northeast corner of Tiverton Basin at Mackerel Cove, under the projection of the railroad bridge.

The Fall River Yacht Club, *c.* 1908. The yacht club counted among its members people from Portsmouth as well as Tiverton.

The Fall River Yacht Club, *c.* 1912. Across the quiet Sakonnet River, summer cottages huddle along Portsmouth's Hummocks' shore; the menhaden fisheries are at far right.

Howland's Ferry seen from above the Tiverton approach to the old Stone Bridge, from a postcard dated October 12, 1906. A cluster of fishermen's shanties and cottages line the shore along Riverside Drive north and south of the railroad station.

The ferry *West Side* at its Portsmouth slip. The *West Side* and the *J.A. Sanders* were pressed into service in 1907 while the Stone Bridge was being strengthened.

A dated O.E. Dubois photograph. The ferry *West Side* approaches its temporary slip and dock. Notice the work boat near the Stone Bridge.

The steamboat *Queen City*, *c.* 1900. Pierce's Wharf was used by several steamers providing daily service for thirty years between Sakonnet Point and Providence, making stops at Fogland, Stone Bridge, and Bristol Ferry. Captain Julius A. Pettey, a local resident, bought the *Queen City* and began running her in 1887.

Lawton House (*c.* 1750–1854). This *c.* 1907 photograph shows the large, two-and-a-half-story building with its brick center chimney and balustrade Colonial Revival central entry. The house, set on a small landscaped lot, was the Lawtons' home for more than 150 years.

Barker's Outlook, *c.* 1900. This is a large and elaborate, two-and-a-half-story, early-twentieth-century Colonial Revival residence with extensive porches and balustrade hip roof. It commanded an excellent view to the west, and was at one time the home of Richard Jackson Barker, son of Benjamin Barker. The Barkers operated a Fall River lumber business. Barker's Outlook was destroyed by fire around 1989.

Tiverton's first soft ice cream stand, Gledma's Dairy Dip, 1088 Stafford Road, *c.* 1955. Ed St. Amour and his wife, Mary, founded the business in 1955. Gloria Desrosiers, their daughter, is the current proprietor. Mary says they routinely see the children and grandchildren of their regular customers. Displaced "Tivertonians" visiting their old hometown drop by the stand for a taste of Gledma's flavorful ice cream served with a friendly Tiverton smile.

A North Tiverton commercial block, *c.* 1919. The William Walker shoe and dry goods and Walker Bros. meat and produce stores were located at the busy corner of State and Main Streets.

The rustic lobby and lounge of the Stone Bridge House/Cottages/Inn (1880 et seq.; 1800 Main Road), c. 1905. Captain Lawton built the original Stone Bridge House in 1790; it eventually became a well-known resort. Fire destroyed the building in 1847, but it was rebuilt in 1848. In 1864, Asa T. Lawton purchased the building and reopened it in 1865 as Lawton House. Later in 1865, it was sold again; shortly after the sale, it was destroyed by fire, and was again rebuilt.

Stone Bridge Cottage, *c.* 1905. The building is a large, wood-shingled, two-and-a-half-story hotel and restaurant, occupying a corner lot at the east end of what was once the Stone Bridge. The building is the third on this site. The once-fashionable resort catered to vacationers and travelers for almost two centuries. Notice the open-roofed piazza that went around the building.

The Stone Bridge Inn, November 1996. The greatest exterior change to the 1888 building was the enclosure of the piazza. This building is an important remnant of Rhode Island's late-nineteenth-century development as a seaside resort. Since the mid-1970s several attempts to rehabilitate the facilities have met with limited success at best.

A mass of wreck and ruins on the Tiverton shore. September 21, 1938, is remembered as the date of the disastrous hurricane that swept through New England in a fury of destruction.

Boats and debris piled against the railroad bridge. In its wake, the unnamed tropical storm left a horrible toll. Over six hundred were dead, with more than one hundred persons missing and nearly six thousand homes destroyed. The storm up-rooted tens of thousands of great trees and countless smaller ones, and wrecked untold numbers of boats.

Three
Nanaquaket and Bridgeport

The Nanaquaket Neck Historic District, c. 1907. Nanaquaket Neck is a residential area bounded by the Sakonnet River to the west and the Quaket River to the north. Nanaquaket Pond to the east is an almost landlocked, salt-water pond. The northern end of the neck was originally the home of Pocasset Queen Weetamoe, wife of Alexander, brother of King Philip. Unlike most of Tiverton, which was wooded, the neck included grassland and arable land where the native inhabitants cultivated maize, beans, and pumpkins. The neck of land was sold to Captain Richard Morris of Portsmouth in 1651.

The old Stone Bridge with draw raised on June 8, 1907. The boardwalk along Main Road (Route 77) is precariously close to the Quaket River bank.

A view of the Nathaniel Boomer Church Estate from Main Road on the Quaket River, c. 1907. The property was a wedding gift of George Washington Humphrey to his daughter Mary when she married Nathaniel Boomer Church, one of the seven famous Church brothers. Church's wealth made the Second Empire twelve-room house with its boathouse, pier, large stable, and orchards on the 20-acre lot a grand place.

The Captain Nathaniel Boomer Church estate, c. 1907. Here, the observer is allowed an unencumbered view of the north end of Nanaquaket Neck and the Church property. The property was acquired by the Roman Catholic Diocese of Providence in the 1930s; it is now the convent of the Order of St. James.

A Church family menhaden boat at anchor in the Quaket River, c. 1906. In the middle background (left) is the stone causeway to the wood bridge (center) across the river to Nanaquaket Neck (right). In 1875, George Humphrey received authorization to build a bridge across the strait leading into Nanaquaket Pond. In 1883, a wooden bridge with stone piers and abutments was completed and a public road was laid out along the neck.

A view of Captain Church's boathouse and mansion from Main Road, *c.* 1907. Captain Church built the house in 1872. Mary died in 1879, leaving the captain with three daughters: Elizabeth, Caroline, and Ruth. Not long after Mary's death, he married Rhoda Seabury of New Bedford; the two children of that union were named Nathaniel Jr. and Mary.

A view of the Nanaquaket boathouse from the mansion, *c.* 1907. The Captain was brought up on the sea. His father, Joseph, was a fisherman, and at age ten, Nathaniel started working as a cook on his father's boat. Captain Nat, as he was later affectionately known, was one of seven brothers. He had a sister as well, named Calista.

The original Nanaquaket mansion, c. 1870. Nanaquaket was a magnificent twelve-room house on 20 acres set apart from Tiverton by water on three sides. Eventually, the mansion included separate servants' quarters, a boathouse with a fully equipped dining hall on the second floor, a large pier, and a stable with quarters for a groom.

Captain Nat and his pogy boat skippers at a boathouse banquet, *c.* 1907. The Captain, right of center wearing a black cravat, loved parties—of that there is little dispute. He fitted the second floor of his boathouse with all the amenities needed to prepare and serve a sumptuous repast. He entertained his friends at an enormous circular dining table. A typical menu at one of his

all-male parties included Tiverton Bay oysters, celery, olives, almonds, chicken consomme, Maryland terrapin, mallard duck Nanaquaket, Rhode Island wild rice, Indian corn croquettes, grilled sweet potatoes, Roquefort cheeses, and café noir. The nine courses were accompanied by champagnes, wines, and aperitifs, topped off with cigarettes and corona cigars.

A view of Stone Bridge and the Portsmouth Hummock from Nanaquaket's water tower, *c.* 1907. The building in the foreground is the handsome stable and carriage house.

A water tower view of Quacket Pond, the Bridgeport, and the Sin and Flesh Brook area.

Irrigating the land. This high water tower was capable of delivering water to all of Nanaquaket's buildings and the extensive gardens and orchards.

The Church estate. The Captain was generous in allowing his estate grounds to be used for church and community affairs. The plaques on the entrance pillars reveal an obscure spelling for the place, *Nanaquackett*.

The ladies' retreat. While the captain entertained his pogy boat skippers in the boathouse, Mrs. Church, a proper Victorian hostess, and her guests enjoyed the summer breezes in Nanaquaket's enclosed gazebo. Seen here from left to right are an unknown lady, Caroline Church Luscomb, who is standing behind children Caroline Davis and Louisa Davis Almy, Ruth Church Davis with her son Willard, and Captain Church's wife, Rhoda.

A partial view of Nanaquaket's large subsistence garden, *c.* 1907. The woman shown here with a child is Captain Nat's daughter, Caroline Church Luscomb; the child is Caroline's niece.

Caroline Church Luscomb and her husband, Clifford, at their Tiverton home, 1958.

Captain Nat's gasoline launch moored at the estate's floating dock. The boathouse is being prepared for the arrival of guests for a clambake. West Road is in the background.

The steam yacht *Felicia*, *c*. 1900. United States Senator Nelson W. Aldrich paid frequent visits to Nanaquaket. In 1883, Captain Nat was elected a representative from Tiverton to the Rhode Island General Assembly as a Democrat; he served until 1888. During his tenure, he was on the oversight committee involved in the building of the Rhode Island State House. Later, he was on the commission that built the Stone Bridge, overseeing construction from Nanaquaket's verandah.

The John Gray House and Tavern (pre-1700), *c.* 1935. Gray established one of the first taverns in the area, along the gut in Bridgeport. Later, the house was home to the famous Tiverton fishing family, the Churches; a seine house and perhaps a fish factory were located adjacent to the house.

Fourth-grade scholars of the Bridgeport Grammar School, 1918. From left to right are as follows: (front row) Rose Neronha, Janice Grinnel, Annie Rose, Mabel Grinnel, Mildred Rose, Pearl Lewis, Florence Fitzlet, and Dorothy Negus; (middle row) Ruth Simmons, Margaret Cotteral, Norman Francis, Melvin Sanford, Robert Burrell, and Manuel Neronha; (back row) Leslie Delano, Abbie Rose, Goodwin Delano, Willard Davis, Carl Wilcox, Lloyd Lawton, Billy Chase, Dwight Hambly, Frank Neronha, and Clarence Bliss.

The gut at Sin and Flesh Brook, east of Nanaquaket Pond, *c.* 1907. On March 21, 1676, John Howland was killed by Native Americans. His body was thrown into a waterway that ran red with his blood; henceforth the brook was known as Sinning Flesh River and later, Sin and Flesh Brook. Sometime around 1700 a sawmill and a gristmill operated along the river.

Sin and Flesh Gut, *c.* 1900. About 1844 a thread mill was built here; it operated until it was destroyed by fire in 1864. Nearby stood a house used as a hospital by the French during the Revolution; in 1970, it was dismantled to be re-erected in Newport.

The so-called Snell Bridge near the end of Sin and Flesh Brook, where it empties into the gut at Highland Road in Bridgeport, *c.* 1907. A sawmill and a gristmill were built along the brook by Moses and Aaron Barker. About 1844, a thread mill was started here by Sylvanus Nickerson. After Nickerson's death in 1857, it was owned by Oliver Chase and Samuel Thurston, who ran it for a few years before it was taken over by Daniel T. Church.

The Snell Bridge area, January 1997. The mill burned about 1864 and was never rebuilt. There was also an icehouse along a dammed pond on the brook. Today, little besides stone ruins and cellar holes remain of the several early and important structures.

The Nathaniel Briggs House (pre-1777) at 68 Indian Point Road, *c.* 1935. The house is a very large, wood-shingled, Colonial farmhouse with several large chimneys, two pediment entries in (the present-day) east front, and a hip roof with small hip-roofed dormers. The south part of the house is the oldest. The northern service end was built to replace an earlier kitchen and slave quarters.

The Nathaniel Briggs House south doorway, *c.* 1935. The doorway design is another of the very unusual and architecturally interesting local types. It is elaborate and contains some of the same elements, particularly the suggestion of pilasters on each side of the opening framework that have no relation to any supported entablature.

The mantle of the Nathaniel Briggs House, c. 1935. The house once belonged to Colonial Lieutenant Governor Oliver, a Loyalist; after he fled to England, the place was confiscated. It is one of the few remaining old manor houses of the region. In its grand style, it reflects something of the vanished life and atmosphere of the old New England plantations.

The Colonel David Durfee House (1826), 2698 Main Road, *c.* 1935. This is a two-and-a-half-story Federal farmhouse with a large brick center chimney. The fine central entry is distinctive because of its traceried transom light, as well as its extreme height and narrow proportions. This house was the residence of David Durfee, who was a representative in the Rhode Island General Assembly.

Four

Four Corners

The Andrew P. White Store (1876), 3883 Main Road. The White Store was a two-and-a-half-story commercial building with a bell-cast mansard roof, cupola, and a bracketed cornice one-story porch across the front and part of one side. White ran the mill and an icehouse at nearby Pittsville; for a while, this building also housed a post office. The building was restored in 1982.

Tiverton Four Corners, *c.* 1905. The A.P. White Store is at left. In the late 1600s, the proprietors of Puncatest laid out lots extending from the Sakonnet River east to Acoaxet. In 1683, a 4-rod highway was laid out north of Four Corners, following the original trail along the course of the west road Main Road. The village of Tiverton Four Corners was begun about 1710, partly as a result of the earlier settlements along the Sakonnet shore.

Four Corners, November 1996. In 1710, the area was measured and bounded an 80-acre mill lot, including a mill owned by Joseph Taber. At that time, the mill and village were called "Nomscot" for the pond now called Nonquit. Thirty building lots were also measured; these constituted the nucleus of the village of Tiverton Four Corners.

Main Road at Four Corners, looking north, c. 1905. The Amicable Congregational Church at 3736 Main Road (left) is a small Greek Revival church built in 1845; this is the second Congregational church building on this lot. The church parsonage at 3804 Main Road (middle) is a one-and-a-half-story vernacular structure built in 1832. In the right foreground is 3832 Main Road, the Templar's Hall/Union Library, built in 1868.

The same location as above, November 1996. The Union Public Library is a simple one-story, wood-shingled building, set gable end to the road. The library society, founded in March 1820, is the oldest in Tiverton and second oldest in Newport County. Except for the paved highway and sidewalk, and the thick growth of trees, little else has changed here since the nineteenth century.

The Amicable Congregational Church (1845–1846 et seq), *c.* 1896. This church was a small but monumental Greek Revival building with a square, one-stage belfry and three stained-glass windows. Later, it had a large polygonal bay in front flanked by double-door entries.

The Amicable Congregational Church, *c.* 1907. The building is set close to the road on a small lot. The Amicable Congregational Society was organized in 1746, and a church building was erected on Lake Road in 1747.

The Amicable Congregational Church, *c.* 1958. In 1805, this half-acre lot was given to the society to use as a meetinghouse site, and about 1808 the new church edifice was built here. Services alternated between the two buildings until 1844, when the original church building was closed.

Victim to fire. In 1845, the 1808 meetinghouse was destroyed by fire, but was immediately rebuilt according to plans submitted by Pardon Seabury. Since then, the building has been remodeled several times. The building as seen today is an impressive structure commanding the attention of every passerby.

The Arnold Smith House (*c.* 1750/1820 et seq), 3895 Main Road, November 1996. This is a small, shingled, gambrel-roofed cottage with a central entry, with a four-light transom in a three-bay facade. The house, built in 1750, is set on a slight rise. About 1820, an addition—a long, one-and-a-half-story ell—was made at the west side (rear); later, the center chimney was removed.

The Chase-Cory House (*c.* 1730 et seq), 3908 Main Road, Tiverton Historical Society Museum, November 1996. This is a gambrel-roofed cottage with a large brick center chimney, a four-light transom over the central entrance, an asymmetrical, four-bay façade, and an ell at the rear. It is one of the best-preserved examples of a modest Colonial farmhouse to be found in Tiverton.

The A.P. White Gristmill (c. 1850), 3946 Main Road, shown here c. 1905. This one-and-a-half-story masonry building with stuccoed stone sides has a central, double-door entry in the gable end. In this photograph the sign above the door announces: "A. Peregrine White, Est. Jan. 1, 1866." The building was used as a gristmill that ground corn for Rhode Island jonnycake meal. The miller lived in the house next to the mill.

The A.P. White mill race and long unused water wheel, c. 1905. This was the site of a 1710 sawmill and gristmill that was abandoned before 1847. The mill shown here is either new or a restoration of the original. The figure of a well-dressed gent seated to the right of the arch gives scale to the surroundings. Suspicion is that the figure is that of the photographer, O.E. Dubois.

The Chapel of the Mission of Holy Trinity (Episcopal), *c.* 1905. In 1712, Reverend James Honeyman of Newport was appointed to minister to the Episcopal faithful of Tiverton. Services were conducted at several places in the Stone Bridge-Bridgeport area until 1890, when a chapel was consecrated near the railroad station. In 1915, the church bought land on Main Road and in 1917 the first services at the Holy Trinity Episcopal Church were held.

Traveling north on Highland Road, *c.* 1909. The tower of the Central Baptist Church (1887) is on the right horizon.

The Old Stone Church/First Baptist Church (1841), 5 Old Stone Church Road, *c.* 1910. This was a simple, stuccoed, stone meetinghouse, set gable end to the road, with a low, squat tower and a one-story addition at the rear. The plain facade has a pair of entrances and three tall windows at each side. Behind the church is the parsonage (1884), a plain, two-and-a-half-story structure with a flat-roofed, bracketed hood entry.

A Stone Church clam bake, *c.* 1910. The church's clambakes were so popular and well-attended that the town fathers declared the bake-day a holiday. Organized as a Six-Principle Baptist Society in 1680, the church has served faithful from Dartmouth, Tiverton, and Little Compton. The first meetinghouse was erected in 1752. In 1835, the society became Free Will Baptist. The present church was built in 1841.

The Old Tavern, *c*. 1903. Called Connly's Tavern, this two-and-a-half-story building with massive interior hearths and one-and-a-half-story ell was located along Main Road. The size of the structure suggests that it was run as an inn. Built before the American Revolution, it was operated for many years by the Durfee family. The building was torn down sometime between 1902 and 1905.

Five
Little Compton
and Adamsville

A Little Compton country road in winter, dated December 1892. Impressionist painter Sydney R. Burleigh, a prolific painter of watercolors, oils, and Rafaelli colors, was born in Little Compton in 1853 and died in Providence in 1929; his work is widely owned in Rhode Island. A member of the Providence Art Club, Burleigh was its president from 1915 to 1921, and was also the first president of the Providence Watercolor Club. In 1885, he built his landmark studio, the Fleur de Lis, on Thomas Street in Providence. (R.V. & I.V. Simpson collection.)

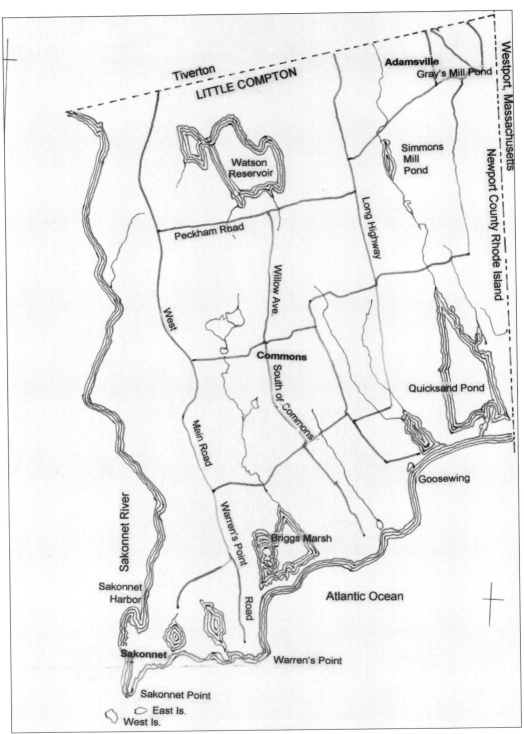

A detail map of Little Compton.

The Rhode Island Red Monument (1925), the world's only such tribute to a chicken. This monument consists of a large granite boulder with a bronze tablet bearing the likeness of a chicken and the inscription: "To commemorate the birthplace of the Rhode Island Red breed of fowl which originated near this location." The breed originated at William Tripp's farm on Long Highway.

Chicken for sale. The marker was probably placed here because many of these birds were purveyed at Manchester's Store just across the street. The Manchesters donated the land for the marker, no doubt as a clever marketing ploy. This monument remains the most popularly known landmark in Adamsville.

The Church-Manchester Store (*c.* 1820), as seen in 1950. To the right is the so-called Spite Tower. Ebenezer P. Church came from Fairhaven, Massachusetts, in 1818 and he built this general store in 1820. Philip Manchester became Church's partner in 1838; he became full owner in 1864, and the store remained owned and operated by the Manchester-family until the 1960s.

The Church-Manchester Store, Main Street, *c.* 1930. This imposing early-nineteenth-century, two-and-a-half-story clapboard building stands gable end to the street. At the rear stands a modern ell that connects the main structure to a one-story wing on the west that originally stood alone. A one-story country-style porch stretches the full width of the facade. Now operating as a restaurant, it maintains the Manchester name.

Rugged stone fences define property lines, looking northeast c. 1911. The village of Adamsville, at the northeast corner of the town, is separated from the rest of Little Compton by Colebrook Woods. Nestled in a valley at the convergence of several roads and at the head of the Acoaxet River, it sprawls across two towns, Little Compton and Westport, Massachusetts.

Looking southwest from Adamsville Road in Westport. Except for the elimination of the dirt road seen in this c. 1911 photograph, today this area retains much of its provincial charm. Adamsville is as it always has been primarily residential. The village, with its winding roads lined with ancient stone fences and neat green-shuttered white houses, remains a place of peace and quiet.

Adamsville Mill Pond, c. 1910. As early as 1750, this was the site of a gristmill, and by the early nineteenth century a sawmill and a carding mill also stood here. Little Compton's first post office was established here in 1804. By the mid-nineteenth century, there were some twenty homes, the mills, a smithy, two stores, Gray's and Manchester's and Dr. White's drug store, in his home at 35 Main Street.

Only 11 miles to Fall River from this Adamsville milepost at the intersection of Routes 81 and 179 (c. 1910). The predominant Little Compton house form of the eighteenth and early nineteenth centuries is the rectangular-plan, one or two-story houses with gable roofs. In the second half of the eighteenth century, the entrance was often framed with a pediment surrounded by a five-light transom window over the door. Toward the end of the century, semicircular fanlights were used in place of transom lights. Narrow sidelights flanking the door began to appear in the early 1800s.

66

Site of Borden's, Crandall's, and Waite's Mills (at the corner of Main Street and Adamsville Road), *c.* 1940. A stone and earth dam at Adamsville Brook holds back a small, shallow pond. The Benajah [*sic*] Borden gristmill was situated here. Buildings that can be seen here include a large two-and-a-half-story barn, the front porch of Gray's Store, the Samuel Church House, and Spite Tower (center).

Adamsville Brook dam, February 1997. Another mill—a sawmill—was built upstream and later moved here by Stephen Crandall. Both mills on the same lot were later acquired by Benjamin H. Waite, who also powered his mill with this energy source. The building at left is Gray's Grist Mill that operated until 1920. The building in the center serves as professional office space, and at the far right is Gray's Store.

Gray's Grist Mill, February 1997. The mill's owners included David W. Simmons and Philip J. Gray in 1865; Philip J. Gray in 1867; and Otis L. Simmons in 1872. In 1888, the mill came into the hands of the Wilbur family.

The hay scales (right) on Main Street, diagonally across from the Rhode Island Red Monument, *c*. 1930. On this post was a scale containing balances. In front of it was a platform on which wagons hauling coal, wood, hay, or ice were weighed before going to market. Note the magnificent century-old linden trees. In the background is Gray's Store and two-and-a-half-story barn (see p. 67).

Gray's Store (1788) and Little Compton's first post office (1804), seen here *c.* 1927. Gray's is the oldest continuously operated general store in the United States. The current proprietor is Grayton T. Waite, the sixth generation in a family of storekeepers.

The interior of Gray's Store, February 1997. An old-fashioned post office service counter and mail delivery boxes occupy a corner of the store. The post office area doubled as the store owner's business office. Period letters and records are on display.

Gray's Store, *c.* mid-1920s. Built in 1788 by Samuel Church, the store is a living testament to the turn-of-the-century "supermarket." Today, sharing shelf space with the necessaries of olden days are modern convenience goods.

Gray's Store, February 1997. Visitors to Gray's are transported to another time. The store contains the old post office, a marble pump-style soda fountain, antique candy and tobacco cases, and an ice chest. To the right is the Samuel Church House (1815). Church came to Adamsville from Fairhaven early in the century and established a salt works nearby.

The so-called Spite Tower (c. 1905) on Westport Harbor Road, shown here in February 1997. At the rear of the Samuel Church House is this three-story shingled tower with sloping walls and a low hip roof. The structure is built over a well. The tower serves as a well head, with the pump on the first floor, the tank on the third, and chauffeur's quarters on the second.

Spite Tower, c. 1920. Samuel Church died in 1815, in an accident at his salt works. His heirs sold the property to four buyers, who retained it until it was bought by Thaddeus H. Church in 1851. Thaddeus lived in Mobile, Alabama, where he was a cotton merchant. After his death in 1905, the property passed to his niece, Claudia Church Hathaway.

An earlier time. A dusty corner in Gray's Store retains nostalgic reminders of bygone days. A perplexing anomaly concerning Samuel Church is that his age in the year of his death (1815) is always reported to be thirty-three or thirty-five. If this is true, he built his 1788 store when he was only six or eight years old.

Six
Around the Commons

The Grange Hall (1902), Number 8 Schoolhouse (*c.* 1845), and town hall (1880–82), in a *c.* 1910 photograph. The Little Compton Grange No. 32 was established in 1894 with forty-nine charter members. The No. 8 School served in that capacity until the completion of the Wilbour School in 1929. This town hall building superseded the original 1692 building; it is now connected, at the rear, to the Number 8 School. The seventeenth-century Commons is located centrally, and it remains the pre-eminent village within the town since its creation. The civic role of the Commons was intensified as new buildings were built around its periphery through the nineteenth century. The meetinghouse and the Congregational church were supplemented by the Methodist church, stores, blacksmith's shops, and civic buildings. The town's second post office opened here in 1834.

Old Methodist Church faithful gathered after services for this family portrait, c. 1930. Ida Bixby Elwell loaned the photograph and identified, to the best of her recollection, the folks pictured. The first boy standing in the front at the left is George Tubman, and to his left is his brother, followed by four girls: Flossie Buxton, Eleanor Cornell Carroll, Ruth Carter, and Florence Dora Seibel. One of the two basket boys is Franklin Davis. In rows two, three, four, and five, are, from left to right, as follows: (second row) Mabel Bixby (holding John Wordell), Aunt Hattie, Maggie Bixby, Sidney Wordell, Charles Buxton, Myrtle Cory, Etta Brownell (seated), Mrs. Borden, Elizia Bixby (holding Mary Gagnon Harding), Mary Gagnon, Ella Bullock,

and Manuel Sylvia; (third row) Freddie Hatton, Billy Snell, Walter Sylvia, Nelson Wordell, Stanley, Walter Bixby, Albert Wordell, Ida Wordell, Charlette, Alice, Inez, Bertha Davis, Mattie Syble, Dot Childs, Anne Read, Nella Brownell, Ida Elwell, John Jewell, Ida Wilbur, Mr. Tubman (superintendent of schools), Frances Davis, Helen Flynn, and Delma Pool; (fourth row) Emma Fremont Wilbur, Ella Hart, two unknown people, George Bixby, Reverend Clayton B. Small (1928–31), Raymond Peckham, and Laura Sisson; (fifth row) five unknown people, Betty ?, one unknown, George Tubman, Emma Tubman Franklin, two unknown, Ruth Carter, one unknown, and Florence Syble.

The Methodist church (1872), seen here *c.* 1910. This building was across the street from the original 1840 structure, at the west end of the common. This church edifice, severely damaged by the hurricane of 1944, was subsequently demolished; by this time the Methodists had joined the Congregationalists in worship. To the right is the Union Cemetery (1850).

South of Old Burying Ground, *c.* 1907. In the right foreground is the projecting central pavilion of the United Congregational Church. The Methodist church is in the center at the west end of the burying ground.

The United Congregational Church (1832, 1871, 1974, 1986), seen here *c.* 1907. The United Congregational Church was a white clapboard building, three bays deep, set on a high basement with a projecting central pavilion, tower, and spire on the facade. The Modern Gothic detail on the tower and spire date from 1871. The tall spire serves as a town landmark, and is visible from many parts of town.

The interior of the United Congregational Church, *c.* 1907. The Congregational Church has always been an important institution in Little Compton. Indeed, American Congregationalists believed—as did the British before them—that the role of the church included civic authority.

A view to the east on South of Commons Road, C.R. Wilbur's Store at Number 2, *c.* 1905. Charles W. Wilbur with friend and partner William Wood bought the storefront on the Commons on July 4, 1893, from Maria Richmond, who also ran a small store there. Four years later, Wood went to Fall River to run a fish market, and Wilbur purchased his share.

A view to the west on South of Commons Road, *c.* 1914. This area saw leisurely, rural living during the first quarter of the 1900s. Wilbur's Store is at the left, and the Mrs. Wilbur House (*c.* 1860) is facing it. Mrs. Wilbur was living here by 1862. This house is typical of rural Rhode Island domestic architecture of the mid-nineteenth century: it retains traditional forms but embellishes them with new, machine-cut trim.

Seven

The Old Commons Burying Ground

A Dubois photograph of the old tombs, c. 1910. The earliest of these date to the seventeenth century, and the cemetery includes a number of slate markers, both vertical slabs and ledger stones. This is the final resting place of several figures prominent in Rhode Island history, including Elizabeth Alden and Benjamin Church.

The monument encasement of the original Elizabeth Alden Pabodie headstone (June 1882). Elizabeth was the first white child born in New England (1623). Mrs. Sarah Soule Wilbour was the guiding force in the construction of this monument dedicated to the daughter of John Alden and Priscilla Mullins.

A closer view of the Pabodie monument. Mrs. Wilbour noted in her diary: "We went to see the monument put up yesterday. . . . It is a great satisfaction to me to know that the thing is done. I have had it on my mind for 35 years. I started a subscription for the purpose in 1847. . . ."

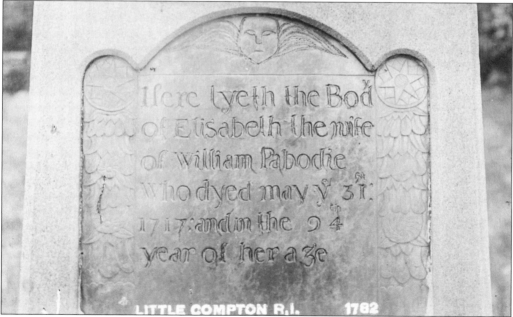

Pabodie's epitaph. The inscription on the original 1717 stone reads: "Here lyeth the Body of Elisabeth the wife of William Pabodie who dyed may ye 31st: 1717: and in the 94th year of her age."

Edward Richmond. Another ancient grave marker gives testament to the passing of Edward Richmond. "The body of Edward Richmond Capt who depated this life in ye 68 year of his age Novem,br [*sic*] 1696."

Cause to wonder. Unusual messages on ancient New England headstones are not unique. However, these two inscriptions give one pause for conjecture. They read: "In memory of Elizabeth who should have been the wife of Mr. Simeon Palmer who died aug 14 1776 in the 64th year of her age" and "In memory of Lidia ye wife of Mr. Simeon Palmer who died Dece'm ye 26th 1754 in ye 35th year of her age."

Memorial Day exercises at Union Cemetery (founded in 1850), 1930. Notable historic markers here include the town's Civil War monument (above) and a full-body, bronze sculpture of Colonel Henry T. Sisson (right, below).

Honor guard for the 1930 Memorial Day exercises. The guard members included Howard Peckham, R. Manchester, and A. Wardell.

Representatives of the Little Compton American Legion at the 1930 Memorial Day exercises. From left to right are Ralph Brownell, Leonard Sylvia, Charles Carter, Everett Barker, Nate Wilbur, Harold Winer, Chester Cray, and Ernest Gifford.

Eight
Architectural and Historic Landmarks

The Betty Alden House (c.1690, 1765, 1890), seen here c. 1910. The Betty Alden House was a shingled, two-and-a-half-story dwelling with a center chimney and asymmetrical facade with a center entrance. William Peabody (1664–1744) built this house about the same time his father built a house nearby at 521 West Main Road.

The Betty Alden House, *c.* 1936. Peabody's grandson John (1700–1767) sold the house to Pardon Gray (1737–1814) in 1762, and the Grays soon added the portion of the house west of the front door. The two-story bay window on the west side, designed by Sydney Burleigh, was added at the end of the nineteenth century.

The Betty Alden House sitting room, *c.* 1910. This house is popularly associated with Elizabeth Alden Peabody (1623–1717), daughter of John Alden and Priscilla Mullins. The attribution is due to the seventeenth-century appearance of the homestead as well as the possibility that Elizabeth lived here with her son after her spouse died in 1707.

The Betty Alden House cooking hearth, *c.* 1907. This structure retains much of its original integrity; it is an important Colonial homestead.

The Friends Meetinghouse (1815), 234 West Main Road, seen here *c.* 1910. This is a plain, shingled, two-story building with a symmetrical four-bay facade, two off-center entrances, and paired interior end chimneys. Quakers in Little Compton established their communion in 1700, assisted by Dartmouth and Portsmouth Friends. The first meetinghouse stood on this site, and portions of it were incorporated into the present building.

Old Acre, the Church-Burchard House (*c.* 1841, 1890), 420 West Main Road, seen here *c.* 1910. This is a large, elaborate, and handsome Colonial Revival house, two-and-a-half-stories tall with a full-width one-story porch that includes a pediment over the center entrance. Chinese Chippendale balustrades ornament the roof. Broad, deep, projecting bow windows are featured on the principal elevations.

The Bailey Homestead (early to mid-nineteenth century et seq), 55 Sakonnet Point Road, seen here c. 1913. This is a two-and-a-half-story, shingled farmhouse. The house has had several additions to both sides and rear, which were added when needed and made possible by wealth. The house stands on land owned since the seventeenth century by the Bailey family.

"Sakonnet House" (the Richmond House and the Sakonnet Golf Club, c. 1850 et seq.), 716 West Main Road, seen here c. 1940. This is the oldest structure associated with the emergence of Little Compton as a summer colony; as early as the 1850s the building operated as a country inn. Isaac B. Richmond operated a hotel in the building during the nineteenth century. Before the golf club was organized in 1909, summer residents and hotel guests used the surrounding acres as golf links.

Peggoty, the Sidney R. Burleigh studio, c. 1915. The enclosure is built over the hull of a small cat boat that once acted as a ferry from Little Compton to Middletown. In 1906, after being abandoned for several years, the old boat was hauled by Burleigh to his garden, where he built the superstructure, thatched it, and named it Peggoty. It is now sheltered by a lean-to on the grounds of the Little Compton Historical Society.

The so-called Burleigh Gate, c. 1915. This rustic, handmade gate, designed and crafted by S.R. Burleigh, welcomes visitors to his Little Compton residence.

The Brownell House (eighteenth century, 1823), 1 Meetinghouse Lane, seen here c. 1917. This one-and-a-half-story, center-chimney house has a center entrance framed with sidelights. To the north, a one-story wing is in the same plane as the facade. The exterior of this house resembles an early-nineteenth-century house consistent with the 1823 date.

The interior of the Brownell House, c. 1917. By 1850, this was the home of Town Clerk Deacon Otis Wilbor. Since 1915, when the place was given to the Village Improvement Society, it has functioned as a community center.

Brownell Cottage, on the Commons, c. 1907. This handsome divided stairway is unusual for the period, and is featured in the 1936 *Monograph Series* of early American architecture.

A large rambling house (*c.* 1680, mid-eighteenth century?, 1880), shown here *c.* 1915. Later construction during the nineteenth century produced its present form. The house is a two-and-a-half-story, clapboard building with a five-bay facade, center entrance within an ordinary one-story porch, wide bay windows flanking the entrance, and interior end chimneys.

Pachet (Paget) Brook. This brook about one-quarter mile east of Windmill Hill flows northwest into the Pachet Brook Reservoir and then into the effluent of Nonquit Pond. The reservoir is part of the Newport Water Company's water supply.

Treaty Rock. Beyond the hedgerow (in the center) may be seen the flat outcropping of the ledge called Treaty Rock. This is part of Treaty Rock Farm; in the distance are haystacks and the Sakonnet River.

A touchstone of permanent European settlement in the area. Treaty Rock is a natural outcropping that marks the spot tradition says is the location of the signing of the 1676 peace pact between the aboriginal Sakonnet people and Benjamin Church.

A May 1940 view of Treaty Rock Farmhouse's one-and-three-quarter-story ell (c. 1865). The farmhouse was a two-and-a-half-story dwelling with a five-bay façade and a center entrance within a one-story pediment porch of twentieth-century origin. This house built in the mid-nineteenth century by William H. Chase replaced a seventeenth-century house that was destroyed by fire.

Treaty Rock Farmhouse and its outbuildings, May 1940. The land surrounding this house was settled in the seventeenth century by John Richmond (1594–1664). Richmond then left Little Compton for South County, where the town of Richmond bears his name. Richmond's family stayed at Treaty Rock Farm until the mid-twentieth century.

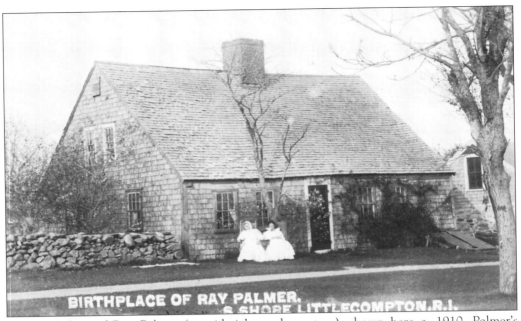

The birthplace of Ray Palmer (c. mid-eighteenth century), shown here c. 1910. Palmer's birthplace was a one-and-a-half-story shingled, center-chimney cottage with a not-quite-symmetrical facade and center entrance. The message on this August 20, 1913, postcard reads, ". . . this old house is on the place and was the house of the author of the hymn, 'My Faith Looke (sic) up to Thee' and it was written in this house."

The Bailey-Sisson House (late 1700s, early-to-mid-1800s), Sakonnet Point Road, shown c. 1910. Jeremiah Bailey, whose family had extensive property holdings in this section of town, owned this property as early as 1850; Lemuel Sisson (1805–1874) bought it from Bailey. It was Sisson who expanded the house from its original two-and-a-half-story, four-bay facade with center chimney to include two two-story ells.

The Peaked Top School marker (late nineteenth century), seen *c.* 1910. By 1712, the town was divided into four school districts, with sessions held by the schoolmaster alternately among them. Classes were often held in private houses, but at least one schoolhouse was built; the so-called Peaked Top School served the southwest part of town. This stone served as the school's front step.

The Peaked Top School marker with capstone in place, *c.* 1915. The small school building was moved around town several times before it was demolished in the late 1800s. This monolithic slab, built into a stone fence at the corner of West Main and Swamp Roads, marks the school's last location. A reproduction of the original school is located on the grounds of Wilbour House on West Main Road.

The Number 8 School Class of 1919. The Number 8 School was at the Commons, next to the town hall. It later became the American Legion headquarters.

Superintendent of schools. Mr. Tubman surveys the Commons from his vantage point at the Number 8 School, *c.* 1928.

A Methodist church Sunday school class
conducted by Ella Bullock in 1925.

Saturday night fever, 1928 style. These classy
teenagers, Ida Bixby (left) and Helen Flynn,
pause for the photographer before rushing off
to the Saturday afternoon square dance.

The first (1930) graduating class of the Wilbour School. From left to right are Mary Sisson, Hazel Simmons, Elizabeth Lackey, Ida Bixby Elwell, Mammie Green DeSilvera, Edith Williamson, and Ann Bliss. These scholars began their studies at the Number 4 School on West Road; they moved to the Josephine F. Wilbour School at 28 Commons as the school's first class in 1929. When the Number 4 School became redundant, it was purchased by Mr. and Mrs. Clayton Lester for use as a residence.

Nine
Sakonnet Farms

LITTLE COMPTON.R.I.1708.

The entrance to Goosewing Beach at the corner of Long Highway and John Sisson Road. In the center background is the Lemuel Sisson Estate. Set on a long, high peninsula overlooking fields, salt ponds, and the roaring Atlantic, this magnificent site includes a rambling, shingled 1700s cottage, a shingled, two-and-a-half-story, late-nineteenth-century house, and stone barns. The farm was the family seat of the Sissons, who came to Little Compton from Newport in 1816.

Harmony Home Farm, on Long Highway, east of William Sisson Road, c. 1915. Ida Bixby Elwell recalls that her father was born at Harmony Home as she was. Her parents, Walter and Mabel, welcomed people from the city to Harmony Home as summer boarders, and in the winter they took in some of the town's schoolteachers. Ida had two brothers, Howard and Raymond, and an extended family of boarders and her mother's brothers, so she was continually exposed to interesting companionship as she grew up on the family farm.

Harmony Home Farm, 1939. These lads are typical of all farm children; they love to play with the farm equipment as they learn its use. Pictured with the farm's fertilizer spreader are Billy and Richard Manchester, and "driver" Walter Elwell. The farm's harvest was largely produced for the sustenance of the family and boarders.

Haying at Harmony Home Farm, 1917. Ida's grandfather, Horace Bixby, was born at Harmony Home in 1872; his parents were originally from Vermont. Many of the Sakonnet farmers preferred ox teams over horses or mules. This team is guided by, from left to right, Howard Wordell, Warren Wordell, Henry Case, and Mr. Colman.

Postal service. In addition to serving on the farm, Walter also worked as one of the town's two mail carriers; he worked the north end of town and Edith Wordell's father delivered mail in the south part of town.

Harmony Home Farm, *c*. 1932. It wasn't all field and barn labor down on the Sakonnet farms. Here Bill Elwell (left) and Ray Bixby are making ice cream. The Bixbys always had a Halloween party for the family children and neighborhood teenagers.

Harmony Home Farm, 1950. The Fourth of July was always the time for the gathering of the clan for the annual clambake. In this photograph the pit is prepared and Water Bixby (left) is directing construction of the pyre. We may assume that freshly harvested seaweed and clams and all the traditional fixin's are nearby waiting to make their entrance.

Bessie Gray with her calves, *c*. 1912. Although this Dubois photograph carries no identification, we may be assured the location is Little Compton's south shore because the image has a negative number within his Warren's Point and Sakonnet photographs. The pastoral tranquillity of this scene is so idyllic that we feel obliged to publish it here.

Harvesting seaweed along the Sakonnet/Westport shore, *c*. 1908. Harvested seaweed is an important source of natural fertilizer for farmers lucky enough to have shore access. Seaweed rights were prized; they were included in land records as easements across a neighbor's land to gain passage to the shore.

A day at the beach, 1916. Mabel Bixby enjoys an outing at South Shore Beach with, from left to right, Bud Davis, her daughter, Ida Bixby (Elwell), and Frances Davis. Ida says that during the summer her parents organized beach parties once or twice a month for the summer boarders. Mabel Bixby always thought of the annual return of the summer boarders as a family reunion.

Children's pageant, c. 1915. Children of the grammar schools present a Statue of Liberty tableau on this float in a Fourth of July celebration. Generally, the town's children were kept busy and out of mischief with organized husking bees, square dances, family picnics, clambakes, and farm work. Fishing, claming, and lobstering kept the older children employed at healthful and profitable labor during the summer months.

Ten
South Shore Cottages and S'cunnet Point

Little had changed in Little Compton by the mid-nineteenth century. Urban centers, such as Providence and Fall River, were now places of dense commercial and industrial business and wealth. Little Compton's beautiful, tranquil, and isolated location attracted visitors on daily sojourns and seasonal visits. In the summer, these urban dwellers escaped to seashore resorts; the wealthy bought land and built country homes.

Sea Lands, Warren's Point, c. 1915. The earliest group of summer homes, built on Warren's Point, were built by families from New York and the midwest. Little Compton's summer residents introduced a formally planned, self-conscious aesthetic order to the town's physical character. They brought an appreciation of contemporary fashion in architecture and landscape and incorporated these ideas into the vacation homes.

Landsend, Warren's Point, c. 1915. The earliest of Little Compton's summer homes were commodious, shingled affairs, drawing heavily on the architectural forms of Colonial New England. The Alden, Clough, and winter houses at Warren's Point and the Slicer House on West Main Road are typical of the large two and two-and-a-half-story dwellings with wide covered porches.

Sunny Mead, *c.* 1915. Little Compton summer homes from the late nineteenth and early twentieth centuries embodied two themes in American architecture: the Colonial and the picturesque. These ideas guided the construction of new homes and the remodeling of older homes and farm buildings into country retreats.

Oneonta, *c.* 1915. Although many of the summer cottages built in the Vernacular Revival style appear generally unpretentious and may suggest a lack of concern for design, they are in reality superbly well planned for low-key, informal summer living.

The Annie D. (Mrs. Gorham Parks) House (1897–1898), Warren's Point, shown c. 1915. This is a large, two-and-a-half-story shingled house with tall chimneys, a high cross-gable roof, and a wide porch that wraps around three sides of the house facing the ocean. There is a one-and-a-half-story carriage house (left) at the rear of the property.

The Anna K. Cowen House (c. 1887–1890), Sakonnet Point Road, seen c. 1915. This is a large, shingled, two-and-a-half-story, Queen Anne/Colonial Revival house with a cross-gable roof, tall chimneys, irregular fenestration, and a wraparound veranda. On the rear of the property is a one-and-a-half-story shingled, cross-gable roof carriage house, probably contemporary to the main house.

A handsome pair of twin summer cottages (*c.* 1920), Sakonnet Point Road. These symmetrical, squarish buildings play handsomely off each other. Their wide, wraparound verandas are perfect for lounging in the cool Atlantic breezes.

The Watch House, a multi-level, Shingle-style summer inn with a commanding ocean view, *c.* 1910. Sakonnet during the first quarter of the twentieth century was much different than it is today. As one approached the point, the grand Sakonnet Inn and large summer houses and inns loomed along the oceanfront.

A view from the Watch House, *c.* 1912. The well-manicured lawn tennis court is ready to receive the inn's guests. Sakonnet's pastoral serenity may be appreciated in this elevated view of fields and the tidal pool.

A view of the "Point" from the Watch House, *c.* 1912. At the top left is West Island. From the late 1860s to about the first decade of the 1900s, this remote outpost was a retreat for wealthy, big-city sportsmen. It is said there was no better striped-bass fishing anywhere along the Atlantic coast than there was here. The telegraph poles seen here were the first installed in Little Compton; they made a submarine connection to the island. During Prohibition, rumrunners made the clubhouse a storage and distribution point for liquor taken from large mother-ships.

The Atlantic face of the Watch House, *c.* 1909. The area changed and developed in direct relation to the kinds of visitors it attracted. Short-term visitors encouraged the development of hotels, inns, and dining halls. The landed summer residents lived in houses, bought or built, and shared a sense of community.

The Sakonnet Inn (1887), also known as Lyman House, shown *c.* 1915. This large, two-and-a-half-story, shingled inn featured spacious, aerie apartments with ocean views. The inn was built by the Sakonnet Steamboat Corporation as an inducement for vacationers to use the corporation's steamers, *Queen City* and *Awashonks*.

A view of the Sakonnet Inn and summer guest cottages from Macauley's on the outcrop of ledge to the east, c. 1910. The message on this postcard reads, "I have put crosses on the houses that father owns. . . . [Signed] L.G. Getchell."

The Sakonnet Inn dominating the point's skyline, c. 1918. The Davis family operated a boarding house near the hotel. Captain Frank Grinnell boarded the crews of his fishing boats in a large building he owned in the same general area around the hotel.

Gathering shellfish. Bakemaster Owen Manchester and his assistant take a break from the gathering of mussels for the afternoon clambake, c. 1905. Manchester was renowned as the organizer of the finest clambakes around. The road to the Sakonnet Inn passed through the gate to Lloyd's Beach.

The Sakonnet Inn and a cluster of cottages on the rocky shore, c. 1905. Telegraph poles follow the path across Lloyd's Beach to the Lyman Hotel, and the steamboat landing and dining pavilion beyond.

Sakonnet Point, *c.* 1907. The peak of commercial fishing activity was reached in the nineteenth century, and a cluster of fishermen's lodging houses sprang up. This rooming house, called the Tierney Block, featured an attached lunch room. The large building at the rear may be a sail loft or chandlery.

The Davis family's boarding house (right), *c.* 1905. Like other seaside towns in southern New England, Sakonnet Point enjoys weather that is relatively moderate, warmed in winter by the gulf stream and cooled in summer by sea breezes. These conditions played a major part in the area's development as a summer resort.

The inviting pleasures of the bathing beach, *c.* 1905. In the background can be seen Sakonnet House, at the intersection of Warren's Point and Sakonnet Point Roads. Sakonnet House was built around 1866 by the Bailey family. The hotel was attached to the family farmhouse. Unfortunately, the venture was a financial disaster and only operated for a few years.

The dining hall at Sakonnet Point, *c.* 1910. Shore dinners, clambakes, chowder and clam fritters, ice cream, and other fancy desserts drew crowds to this seaside pavilion. From the nearby casino dance hall strains of popular music filtered down to the shore.

The steamer *Islander*, c. 1914. Beginning in 1886, Captain Horatio N. Wilcox operated the ferry run between Providence and Sakonnet Point with the steamer *Dolphin*. The *Dolphin* made calls at Bristol Ferry, Stone Bridge, Newtown, and Fogland. Wilcox's steamer service on the 66-foot *Dolphin* opened the Providence market to farmers in the southeastern part of the state. About one year after Wilcox began his service, Captain Julius A. Pettey and others organized the Sakonnet Steamboat Company. They initiated their service with the 92-foot *Queen City*. Later, they added the 107-foot *Awashonks*; she ran for several years until destroyed by fire in 1901. *Awashonks* was replaced by the 106-foot steamer *Islander*. By 1915, only the *Islander*, owned by Philip W. Almy, made the Providence-to-Sakonnet run. Almy also owned the dining pavilion, and a round-trip ticket on the ferry entitled the bearer to a shore dinner.

The excursion steamer *Favorite* of New York, c. 1910. Small excursion steamers and overnight sleepers such as this one found it more difficult to survive than did day-trippers like the *Islander*, which carried freight as well as passengers.

Another view of the above steamer landing, c. 1910. The *Islander* is preparing to depart. In 1910, the *Islander* left Providence at 9 am on weekdays, at 2:10 pm on Saturday, and at 10 am on Sunday. On the return trip, the *Islander* left Sakonnet at 3 pm on weekdays, at 6:30 pm on Saturday, and at 4 pm on Sunday. On each trip, the steamer stopped at Tiverton and Almy's Wharf.

Sakonnet Harbor and Shaw's Dock, *c.* 1915. Another ferry that ran from Little Compton to Middletown was Taggart's Ferry; this service began operations in the mid-1700s, moving farm produce such as butter, eggs, and poultry to the Newport market. The ferry's produce traffic continued for about 150 years. Taggart's Aquidneck landing was situated at the eastern terminus of Green End Road in Middletown.

The cove at Sakonnet Harbor, *c.* 1917. Recreational and commercial maritime activity played varying roles in Little Compton's economy. In the nineteenth century, the lack of a safe harbor made it difficult to establish a large fleet. In the decades of the 1860s and 1870s, there were about seventy fishing boats working out of Sakonnet.

Sakonnet Harbor, *c.* 1907. In the cove, red-painted fishermen's and lobstermen's shanties, large icehouses, and seine and net storage sheds clustered together. As a village devoted to fishing, Sakonnet has a long history. These bountiful waters were harvested by the indigenous natives and the first white settlers.

Sakonnet fishermen's shanties, *c.* 1908. Independent fish processing and packaging plants as well as a prosperous retail trade thrived here. The Bluff Head Fish Market, seafood restaurants such as the Fo'c'sle, and an annex of Wilbur's store served hungry summer visitors. Alas, this was all swept away by the 1938 hurricane and tidal wave.

Sakonnet Harbor, *c.* 1908. According to the *New Bedford Standard* of April 15, 1862, "the fishermen will take possession of their houses, and locate themselves for a month or two at their fishing village, near the breakwater in Little Compton, on Monday, the 21st, where every arrangement will be made for catching the finny tribe at the moment they commence running."

Sakonnet Harbor, *c.* 1908. The *New Bedford Standard* of April 15, 1862, continues, "It is curious to see with what precision and regularity this laborious, yet lucrative business, is conducted. Each gang has its appropriate position to place their leaders and traps, as drawn in a previous convention of fishermen; so that there is not interference with each other."

Sakonnet fishing boats, *c*. 1940. The 1865 census reported that there were fourteen independent fishing concerns with a combined work force of about 150 men operating about seventy boats out of Sakonnet. Their catch consisted mostly of scup, tautog, rockfish, pollock, and bluefish. The record catch for that year was almost 310,000 pounds of fish.

FISHING BOATS AT SAKONNET, R. I.

Sakonnet fishing boats, *c*. 1920. In 1868, the *New Bedford Standard* reported that the seasonal catch of scup that year was valued at over $160,000, but less than $10,000 in value was expected during the 1869 season. Perhaps the dwindling catch was caused by over-harvesting.

Sakonnet fishermen pulling the trap, *c.* 1930s. The call to the fisherman's life is a noble one. The Sakonnet fleet, vulnerable and exposed, was the victim of heavy damage as the result of two disastrous hurricanes within two decades, in 1938 and 1954.

The Sakonnet Point breakwater, *c.* 1957. Work on the breakwater was completed in 1957. Initial construction began 121 years earlier, in 1836; four years later, 200 feet of stone and gravel were in place. In 1899, another 200 feet were added, and in 1954 an additional 400 feet was authorized and designed by the Army Corps of Engineers.

The Sakonnet Point Lighthouse (1883–84), c. 1956. The crusade to relight the beacon began in 1961, when Carl and Carolyn W. Haffenreffer purchased the lighthouse at auction for $1,300. Now fully restored by a group of volunteers, the Sakonnet Lighthouse is maintained as a historic landmark. The structure is a white conical tower built of brick and iron on a brown cylindrical pier, footed on Little Cormorant Rock at the western end of Sakonnet Point, east of the Sakonnet River. The fixed white light is 68 feet above the sea, and when active it flashes three red lights every sixty seconds. The official relighting ceremony took place at dusk from Lloyd's Beach on Saturday, March 22, 1997.

Acknowledgments

The authors offer their sincere thanks and acknowledge their indebtedness to the sympathetic Tiverton and Little Compton citizens who affirmed their faith in us by loaning valuable family photographs. Truly, without their kind generosity, this volume would not exist.

Special thanks go to Joseph Bains of Braintree, Massachusetts, who trusted to our care his extensive collection of rare O.E. Dubois photo postcards. Fully the bulk of images presented here are done so through the generosity of Mr. Bains.

Gratitude is offered to H. Glenn Reed for the photographs of Captain Nathaniel Boomer Church's Nanaquaket mansion. Mr. Reed's O.E. Dubois photographs were commissioned by Captain Church and have never been previously published. We thank him as well for the use of his Nanaquaket monograph, from which we borrowed extensive text.

We extend our thanks to Grayton T. Waite for the loan of his Gray's Store postcards. We also thank Mr. Waite for taking time to review the Adamsville photograph captions for accuracy.

Thanks to Ida Bixby Elwell for her Methodist church group photograph, Wilbour School graduates image, Harmony Home Farm photographs, and her reminisces of life on the farm.

We also acknowledge with thanks these contributors: Leanne Medeiros for the loan of her book *Jonnycakes & Cream*; Florence Archambault for the Little Compton tercentenary book; and John Medeiros for his Treaty Rock Farm photographs. We thank Arthur Waddicor for the Bridgeport scholars, Sin and Flesh Gut, and buildings under the railroad bridge photographs; and Mary St. Amour for her Dairy Dip photograph. The authors also thank their spouses, Jim Devin and Irene Simpson, for their patience, good humor, and support.

Bibliography

Belko, Vivian. *Historic Adamsville: Its People and Places*. Adamsville Historical Association, 1992.

Brownell, Carlton C., ed. *Notes on Little Compton*. Little Compton Historical Society, 1970.

Federal Writers' Project of WPA. *Rhode Island: A Guide to the Smallest State*. 1937.

Historic and Architectural Resources of Little Compton. Rhode Island, 1990.

Historic and Architectural Resources of Tiverton, Rhode Island: A Preliminary Report. 1983.

Longo, Mildred Santille. *Picture Postcard Views of Rhode Island Lighthouses and Beacons*. Rhode Island Publications Society, 1990.

A *Patchwork History of Tiverton, Rhode Island*. 1976 bicentennial edition.

Stretch, George E., ed. *Three Centuries 1675–1975, Little Compton tercentennial*. 1975.

White Pine Monograph Series. Volume XXII. Tiverton, RI, 1936.

O.E. DUBOIS POSTCARD BIBLIOGRAPHY

Authors' Note: O.E. Dubois, a Fall River photographer, apparently published thousands of postcard views of Bristol County, Rhode Island, and nearby Massachusetts in the early decades of this century. These views include scenes from Fall River, Acoaxet, Westport, Sakonnet, Little Compton, Aquidneck Island, and even Jamestown. The following list classifies these images for the first time by negative number. NUMBERS, SPELLING, AND PUNCTUATION ARE REPRODUCED AS THEY APPEAR ON THE CARDS; BRACKETED COMMENTS ARE THE AUTHORS'.

AQUIDNECK ISLAND — PORTSMOUTH

8	COMMON FENCE PT.
1	COMMON FENCE POINT
3	COMMON FENCE PT.
60	A.G. VANDERBILT FARM
61	A.G. VANDERBILT FARM
63	A.G. VANDERBILT FARM [COWS]
64	A.G. VANDERBILT FARM [SHEEP]
88	GLEN FARM [COWS]
89	GLEN FARM
90	GLEN FARM [HORSES]
64	THE HUMMOCKS
84	STONE BRIDGE
25	FORT BUTTS
26	GRIST MILL
42	ENTRANCE TO R.C. VANDERBILT FARM
44	A.G. VANDERBILT'S FARM [WINTER]
45	HUSKING AT VANDERBILT'S
46	HUSKING AT VANDERBILT'S
48	OLD COPPER WORKS
50	A.G. VANDERBILT RESIDENCE
51	ST. MARY'S CHURCH
56	HEN ISLAND
91	THE FISHERIES
68	MAIN ROAD
70	MAIN ROAD [REPRO]
75	TOWN HALL
77	ST. PAUL'S CHURCH
78	LAFAYETTE HOUSE
80	[EAST MAIN ROAD]
81	ST. ANTHONY'S CHURCH
83	[UNIDENTIFIED CHURCH]
84	QUAKER HILL
85	FRIENDS MEETING HOUSE
86	OAKLAND FARM [PUPPIES]
87	OAKLAND FARM [PIGS]
01	ST. PAUL'S
02	[VIEW OF HOTEL AT BRISTOL FERRY]
04	BRISTOL FERRY
05	TURNPIKE ROAD
08	[POWER COMPANY WHARF]
16	NEAR PARK
19	AT ISLAND PARK
90	VAUCLUSE
93	STONE BRIDGE
94	O'NEIL'S POINT [RHODA E. CRANE]

TIVERTON

5	GOULD ISLAND
3	FROM R.R.BRIDGE
8	BRIDGEPORT HOUSE
2	[COWS IN POND]
5	FROM BAPTIST CHURCH
7	FROM BAPTIST CHURCH
0	SNELL BRIDGE [SNELL FARM, LITTLE COMPTON]
8	OLD TAVERN
9	R.R. BRIDG.
A	S. BRIDGE COTTAGE
	STONE BRIDGE
B	AT STONE BRIDGE
	LAWTON HOUSE
	YACHT CLUB
	F.R. YACHT CLUB
	F.R. YACHT CLUB
	STONE BRIDGE
	PAGET BROOK
	AT NANNAQUAKET [TUGBOAT OR FISHERMAN]
	S. YACHT FELICIA
	S.YACHT FELICIA
	BROOK 4 CORNERS
	MAIN ROAD [COUNTRY ROAD]
	NEAR R.R.STA.TIV.
	RAILROAD BRIDGE
	FROM HUMMOCK
	FROM HUMMOCK
	FROM FERRY SLIP
	FROM HUMMOCK
	FROM HUMMOCK
	FROM HUMMOCK

813	FROM BARKER RES.
815	FROM O'NEAL RES.
816	FROM O' NEILS
818	FROM FT BARTON
819	FROM FT BARTON
823	FROM FT BARTON
824	FROM FT BARTON
831	AT FISHERIES
833	FISHERIES STMRS.
834	FISHERIES STMRS.
835	FROM HUMMOCK
841	BENJ. BARKER RES.
842	TIV FOUR CORNERS
848	STONE BRIDGE
851	F.R. YACHT CLUB
853	A.P. WHITE MILL
858	FORT BARTON
865	STONEBRIDGE JUNE 8, 1907
B869	STONEBRIDGE FERRY JUNE 8, 1907
870	N.B. CHURCH PLACE
872	SUGAR LOAF
874	FROM RR BRIDGE
877	NANANQUAKET
879	STONE BRIDGE 7 1907
885	STONE BRIDGE
889	STONE BRIDGE
893	EPISCOPAL CHURCH
894	BETWEEN THE BRIDGES
895	GOULD ISLAND
1251C	STONE CHURCH CLAM BAKE
1251E	STONE CHURCH CLAM BAKE
1251F	STONE CHURCH CLAM BAKE
1251G	STONE CHURCH CLAM BAKE
1393B	STONEBRIDGE
1455	TIVERTON FOUR CORNERS
1456	TIVERTON FOUR CORNERS
1462	BARKER HEIGHTS
1463	BARKER HEIGHTS
G1463	FROM F.R. YACHT CLUB
I1463	FROM F.R. YACHT CLUB [HUMMONC]

LITTLE COMPTON

1 THRU 15 CHILDREN'S PAGEANT SEPTEMBER 5, 1914

7	G.T. BROWNELL HOMESTEAD
28	ST'R ISLANDER AT SAKONNET
586	SAKONNET POINT [BALANCED ROCK]
1124	LITTLE COMPTON
1125	LITTLE COMPTON
1126	LITTLE COMPTON [ONE HORSE CARRAGE]
1127	LITTLE COMPTON
1128	LITTLE COMPTON
1130	TREATY ROCK
1131	LITTLE COMPTON [RICHMOND HEADSTONE]
1132	ODD FL'S HALL
1133	[PALMER HEADSTONES]
1134	THE BETTY ALDEN HOUSE
1136	LITTLE COMPTON [CHICKENS AND COOPS]
1137	SAKONNET POINT [TREE LINED ROAD]
1139	SAKONNET POINT [LYMAN HOTEL]
1140	SAKONNET POINT [BOATS]
1141	[OX TEAM PLOWING]
1142	LITTLE COMPTON [SHEEP/PINES/STONE WALL]
1144	SEAKONNET [SIC] POINT
1148	LITTLE COMPTON [COUNTRY ROAD]
1149	SAKONNET POINT
1150	SAKONNET POINT
1151	GRANGE HALL LITTLE COMPTON
1153	LITTLE COMPTON [OLD ACRE]
1154	LITTLE COMPTON [METHODIST CHURCH]
1155	LITTLE COMPTON [PABODIE OBELISK]
1155[A]	[GRAVE MARKER, PHOTO HAS WIDE WHITE BORDER]
1157	BETSY ALDEN FIRE-PLACE
1158	FIRST CONGREGATIONAL CHURCH
1159	SAKONNET POINT [FISHING SKIFFS / ROCKS]
1163	BATHING BEACH SAKONNET POINT
1164	WATCH HOUSE
1166	THE BREAKERS [UNIDENTIFIED LOCATION]
1167	SAKONNET POINT [STREET SCENE/COTTAGES]
1169	WARREN'S POINT